Life in a Wetland

By Allan Fowler

Consultants

Linda Cornwell, Learning Resource Consultant,
Indiana Department of Education

Janann V. Jenner, Ph.D.

Sharyn Fenwick, Elementary Science/Math Specialist
Gustavus Adolphus College, St. Peter, Minnesota

P Children's Press®
A Division of Grolier Publishing
New York   London   Hong Kong   Sydney
Danbury, Connecticut

Visit Children's Press® on the Internet at:
http://publishing.grolier.com

Designer: Herman Adler Design Group
Photo Researcher: Caroline Anderson

Library of Congress Cataloging-in-Publication Data

Fowler, Allan.
    Life in a wetland / by Allan Fowler.
       p. cm. — (Rookie read-about science)
    Includes index.
    Summary: A simple description of what a wetland is and what kinds
of life can be found in it.
    ISBN 0-516-20799-7 (lib. bdg.)   0-516-26417-6 (pbk.)
    1. Wetland ecology—Juvenile literature. 2. Wetlands—Juvenile literature.
[1. Wetlands. 2. Wetland ecology. 3. Ecology.] I. Title. II. Series.
QH541.5.M3F685   1998   97-28660
577.68—dc21   CIP
                                              AC

Sabine National Wildlife Refuge, Louisiana

What do you think a
wetland is? Many wetlands
are always covered with
a shallow layer of water.

Some wetlands seem dry on the surface, but they have a lot of water in the soil.

Big Inlet Swamp, Pennsylvani

Rocky Mountain National Park, Colorado

There are many types of wetlands. In a marsh, the ground surface is underwater all—or most—of the time.

Common cattails

A marsh is too wet for trees and shrubs to take root. Grassy plants like cattails, bulrushes, and reeds grow in marshes.

Water lilies and duckweed
often grow on top of
the water.

Water lilies

A swamp is flooded for at least part of the year.

Sucker Brook Swamp, Pennsylvan

Atlantic White Cedar Swamp, Massachusetts

Some trees and shrubs
can grow in swamps.

Adirondack State Park, New York

Swamps and marshes
often form along the
banks of slow-moving
rivers and streams.

You may also find one on the edge of a lake or pond. These are freshwater wetlands.

Okefenokee Swamp, Georgia

A salt marsh sometimes
forms where a river flows
into the ocean.

Deal Island, Marylan

The water level in a salt marsh rises and falls with the ocean tides.

Many fish, shellfish, and other sea creatures live in salt marshes.

Everglades National Park, Florida

Mangrove swamps are salt marshes found in warm places. They are named after the mangrove trees that grow there.

Most trees need fresh water to grow, but mangrove trees thrive in salty ocean water. Their tangled roots reach far above the muddy ground.

Caroni Swamp, Trinidad

Alligators and crocodiles, beavers and otters . . .

American alligator

. . . turtles and frogs, snakes
and salamanders, are among
the many animals that live
in swamps and marshes.

Great blue heron

Long-legged birds like
herons wade along the shore
and through the shallow
waters, looking for fish.

Dragonflies and other insects buzz around.

Red-necked grebe catching a dragonfly

A bog is another type of wetland. Its water does not come from a stream, a lake, or an ocean.

Cape Breton Highlands, Nova Scotia, Canad

Adirondack State Park, New York

Rainwater keeps the soil
in a bog damp and spongy.

Davis, West Virginia

The plant life in a bog
is much simpler than in
a marsh or swamp. Moss
usually covers large areas
of the ground.

When the plants in a bog die, they do not rot away, so layers and layers of dead plants build up on top of each other.

Tahquamenon Falls State Park, Michigan

The weight of the upper layers pushes down on the lower layers.

This turns the plants into a dense, soil-like material called peat.

County Sligo Bog, Ireland

Some people dig up peat
and burn it like wood to
heat their homes.

25

When heavy rains fall
or winter snows melt,
much of the water is held
by wetlands.

Everglades National Park, Florid

By holding the water, wetlands help keep the land around them from being flooded.

People didn't always know that. They drained many wetlands and covered them with landfill.

Now they are trying to save the wetlands that are still left.

In large wetlands like Everglades National Park in Florida . . .

Everglades National Park, Florid

Okefenokee Swamp, Georgia

. . . and the Okefenokee
Swamp in Georgia and
Florida, life goes on as
it always has.

Words You Know

bog

marsh

swamp

wetland

30

alligator

cattails

heron

mangrove tree

peat

water lily

mangrove swamp

salt marsh

Index

About the Author

Allan Fowler is a freelance writer with a background in advertising. Born in New York, he lives in Chicago now and enjoys traveling.

Photo Credits

©: Jonathan Nutt: 6, 7, 31 center right, 31 top center; Photo Researchers: 21 (Peter G. Aitken), 25, 31 center (Bill Bachman), 10 (John Bova), 5, 30 top right (Kent & Donna Dannen), 15 (Gregory G. Dimijian, M.D), 26 (Douglas Faulkner), cover, 4, 8, 20, 30 top left, 30 bottom left (Michael P. Gadomski), 22 (D. Lyons), 12, 31 bottom right, (Robert Noonan), 23 (Rod Planck); Sharon Cohen: 14, 31 center left, 31 bottom left; Tim Laman: 9; Tony Stone Images: 19 (Horst Baender), 3, 30 bottom right (Darrell Gullin), 17 (Bill Ivy), 28 (David Job), 18, 31 top right (Byron Jorjorian), 16, 31 top left (David Muench), 11 (Bob Thomason), 29 (Randy Wells).